Science in Infographics

MATERIALS

Jon Richards
and Ed Simkins

Please visit our website, www.garethstevens.com.
For a free color catalog of all our high-quality books,
call toll free 1-800-542-2595 or fax 1-877-542-2596.

Cataloging-in-Publication Data

Names: Richards, Jon. | Simkins, Ed.
Title: Materials / Jon Richards and Ed Simkins.
Description: New York : Gareth Stevens Publishing, 2020. | Series: Science in infographics | Includes glossary and index.
Identifiers: ISBN 9781538242834 (pbk.) | ISBN 9781538242858 (library bound) | ISBN 9781538242841 (6 pack)
Subjects: LCSH: Materials--Juvenile literature. | Materials science--Juvenile literature. | Information visualization--Juvenile literature.
Classification: LCC TA403.2 R47 2020 | DDC 620--dc23

Published in 2020 by
Gareth Stevens Publishing
111 East 14th Street, Suite 349
New York, NY 10003

Printed in the United States of America

CPSIA compliance information: Batch #CS19GS: For further information contact Gareth Stevens, New York, New York at 1-800-542-2595.

CONTENTS

ATOMS AND MOLECULES

Atoms are the basic building blocks of matter. Atoms combine to make everything in the universe, including your body and enormous, blazing stars.

Atoms

An atom is made up of a nucleus, around which whiz tiny electrons.

Nucleus – the nucleus lies at the center of an atom and it contains smaller, subatomic particles called protons and neutrons.

Electrons – these are found whizzing around in shells around the atom's nucleus.

Neutrons have a neutral charge.

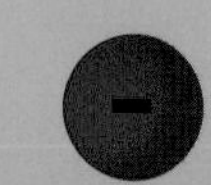

Electrons have a negative charge.

Protons have a positive charge.

Atoms usually have the same number of protons and electrons so that the positive and negative charges are balanced.

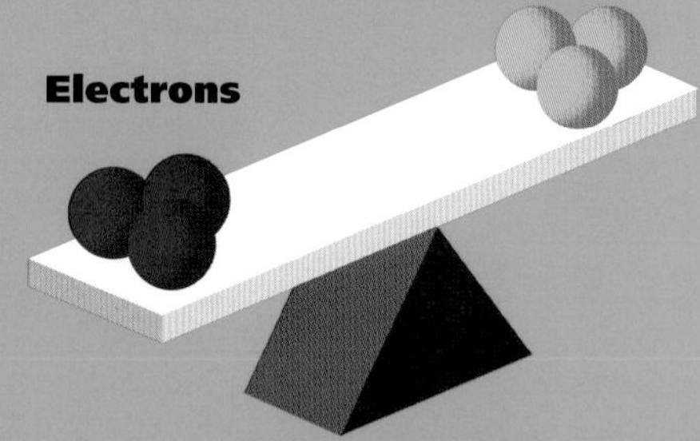

Atomic number

This is the number of protons in an atom and it determines what element the atom belongs to. For example, hydrogen has an atomic number of one, and it has one proton. Carbon has an atomic number of six, because it has six protons.

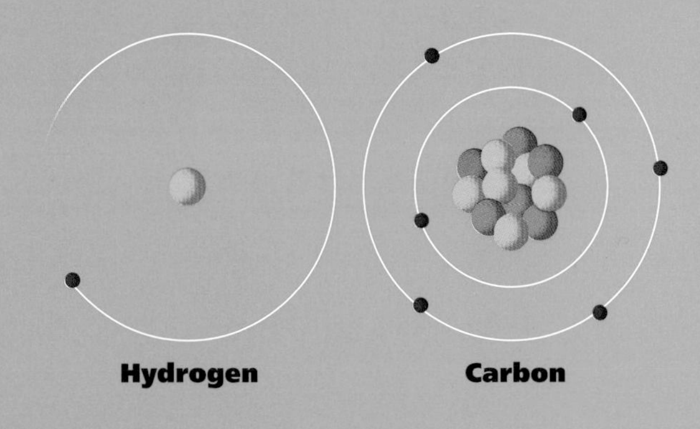

Elements

Elements are made up from only one type of atom.

92

the number of elements found in nature. Scientists have been able to create more than another 20 elements in laboratories.

Periodic table

Scientists use the atomic number to arrange the elements into the periodic table.

H																	He
Li	Be											B	**C**	N	O	F	Ne
Na	Mg											Al	Si	P	S	Cl	Ar
K	Ca	Sc	Ti	V	Cr	Mn	Fe	Co	Ni	Cu	Zn	Ga	Ge	As	Se	Br	Kr
Rb	Sr	Y	Zr	Nb	Mo	Tc	Ru	Rh	Pd	Ag	Cd	In	Sn	Sb	Te	I	Xe
Cs	Ba		Hf	Ta	W	Re	Os	Ir	Pt	Au	Hg	Tl	Pb	Bi	Po	At	Rn
Fr	Ra		Rf	Db	Sg	Bh	Hs	Mt	Ds	Rg	Cn	Nh	Fl	Mc	Lv	Ts	Og
			La	Ce	Pr	Nd	Pm	Sm	Eu	Gd	Tb	Dy	Ho	Er	Tm	Yb	Lu
			Ac	Th	Pa	U	Np	Pu	Am	Cm	Bk	Cf	Es	Fm	Md	No	Lr

Carbon is shown using the letter C and has an atomic number of 6.

Molecules

Atoms join together to form molecules. Molecules can include atoms from one element, or atoms from several different elements.

Oxygen – a molecule of oxygen is made up of two oxygen atoms and is written as O_2.

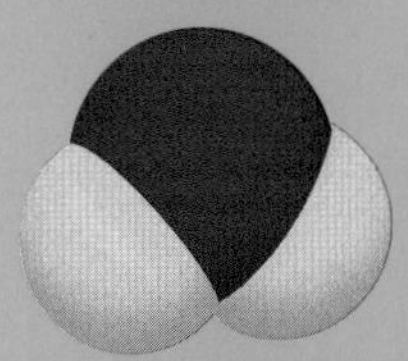

Water – a molecule of water is made up of two hydrogen atoms and one oxygen atom, and is written H_2O.

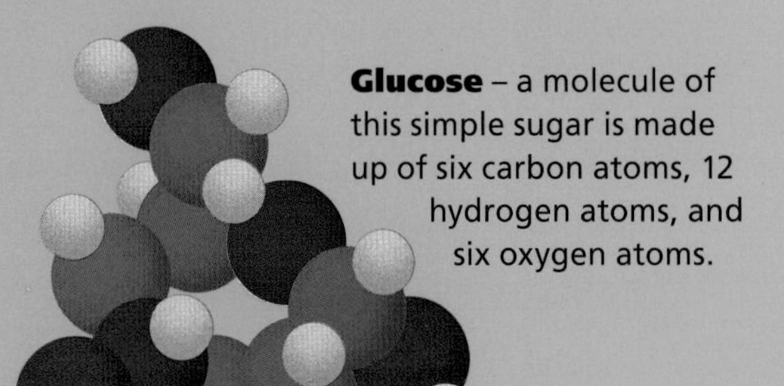

Glucose – a molecule of this simple sugar is made up of six carbon atoms, 12 hydrogen atoms, and six oxygen atoms.

SOLIDS

Matter and materials come in different forms, or states. Something that is solid has a fixed shape, it cannot flow, and it cannot be compressed, or squashed.

Inside a solid

The forces holding the particles together are called bonds.

The bonds between the particles that make up a solid are very strong, which gives it a rigid shape.

Even though they are held together firmly, the atoms of a solid will vibrate, depending on the amount of energy they have.

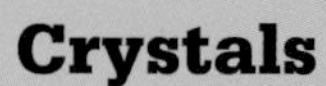

Crystals

These solids have particles arranged in a repeating lattice pattern. For example, sodium (Na) and chlorine (Cl) atoms combine in a lattice to form crystals of sodium chloride (NaCl), which is better known as table salt.

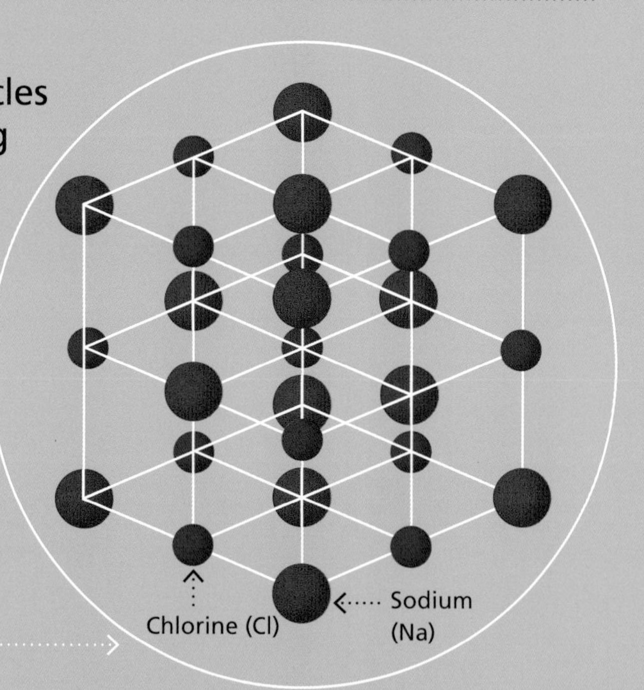

Metals

This type of solid is made up of more than 70 elements. Properties of metals include:

They are solid at room temperature (except Mercury [Hg], which is a liquid at room temperature).

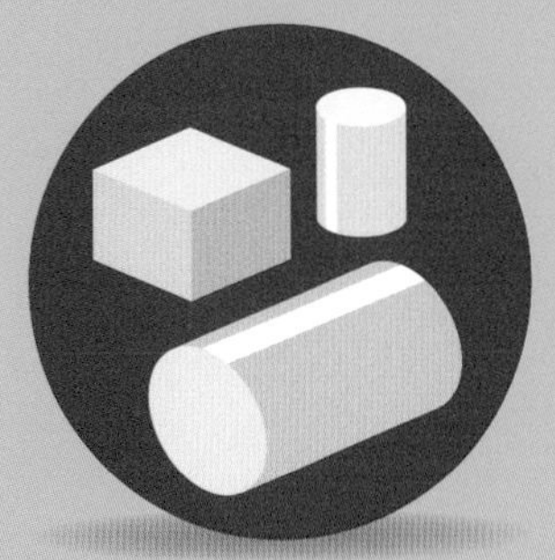

They are usually gray and shiny.

They can be rolled into sheets or stretched to make wire.

They conduct electricity.

MIXING METALS

Metals can be mixed with other elements to make alloys.

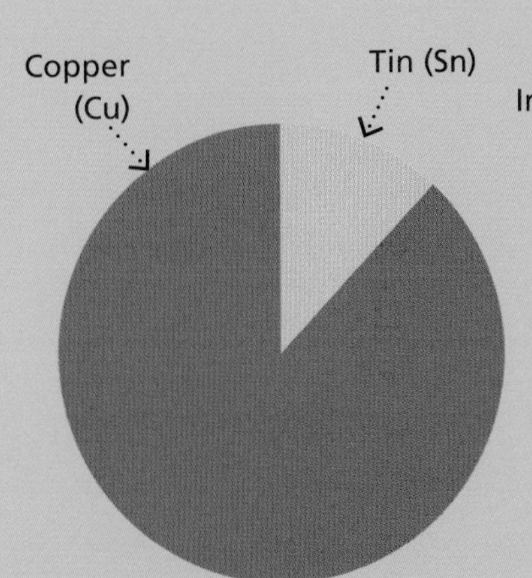

Bronze is an alloy of copper and tin (about 12 percent tin).

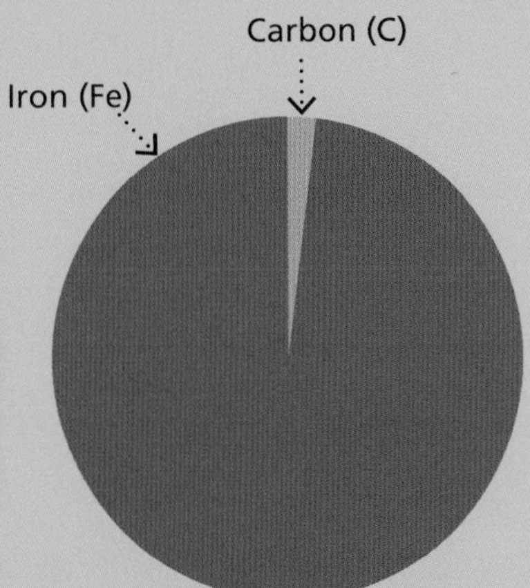

Steel is an alloy of carbon and iron (up to 2 percent carbon).

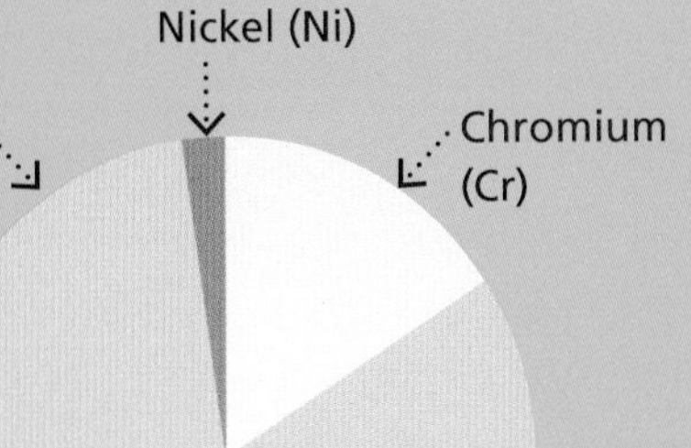

Stainless steel, used to make cutlery and scissors, also contains chromium and nickel.

Ceramics

These are solids that can be made from naturally occurring nonmetals, such as clay and sand.

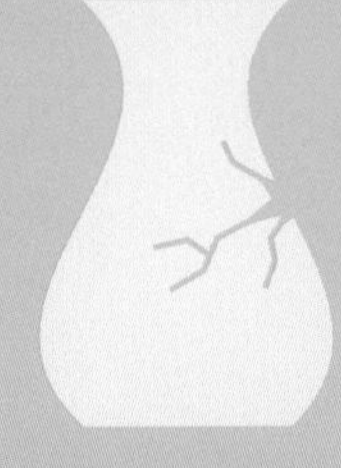

They can be strong, but brittle. They do not conduct electricity.

They have been used for thousands of years to make pots and other storage vessels and crockery. Today, they are also used in computer chips, electrical insulators, pens, and cars.

CARBON

This amazing element appears in a wide range of different forms. It helps us to write and draw, is one of the most valuable substances on the planet, and even forms the basis of all living things.

THE CARBON CYCLE

Carbon moves from one form to another in a cycle. It is found in carbon dioxide, a gas that humans and animals breathe out and plants take in to make sugars. Fossil fuels contain carbon from the bodies of plants and animals that died millions of years ago.

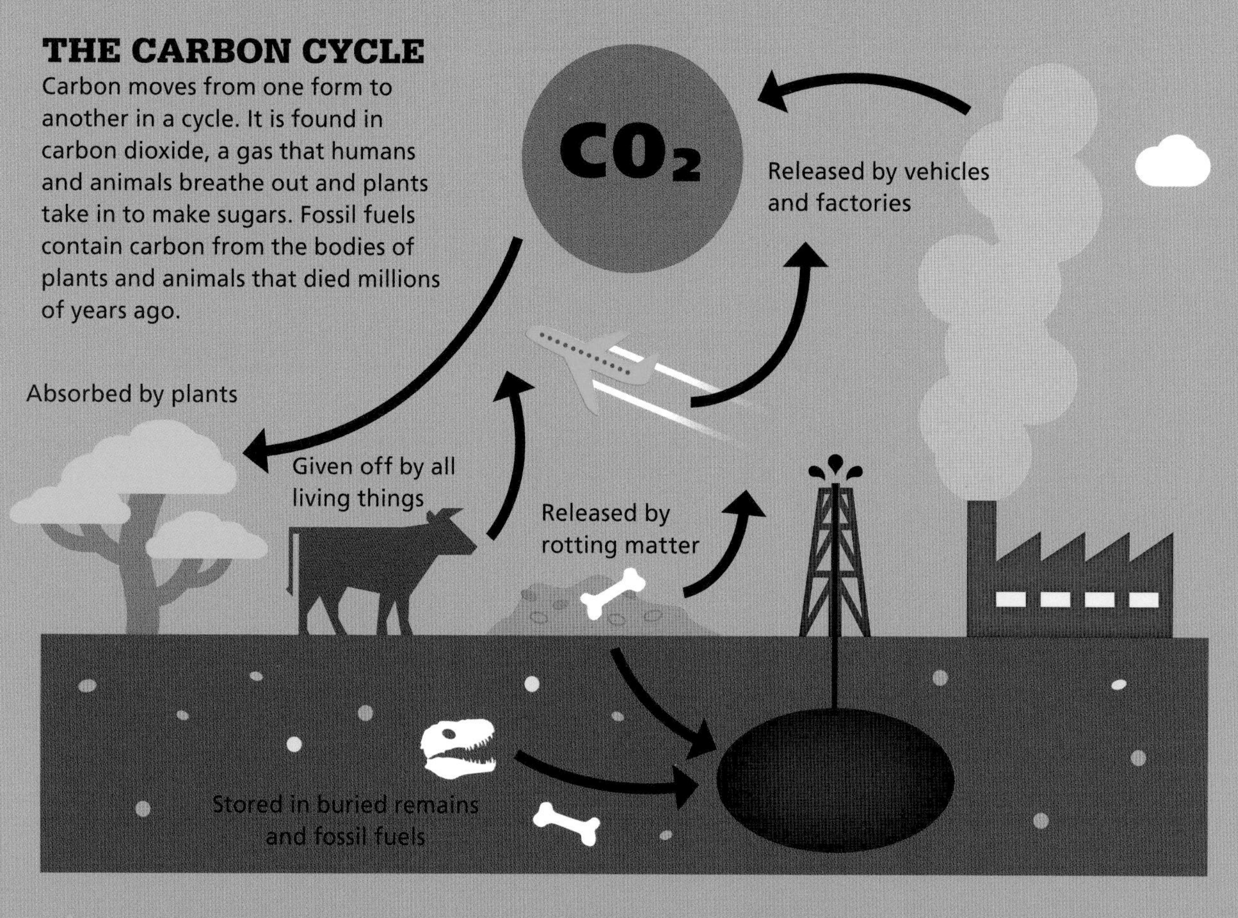

Pencils

Carbon atoms can bond in different ways. One of these is as the mineral graphite. When graphite is rubbed across a surface, it leaves behind tiny crystals, producing dark gray lines.

Graphite

Layers of graphite are loosely bonded together and slide over each other easily.

Graphite is the gray material in the middle of a pencil.

Diamond

If carbon is subjected to high temperatures and enormous pressure, it can turn into a crystal called diamond.

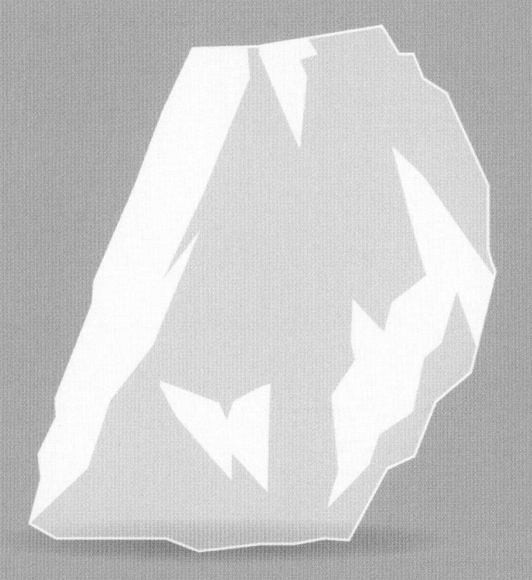

Diamonds can be cut to produce sparkling diamond jewelry.

Diamonds are weighed using units called carats. **A carat is equivalent to 0.2 gram.**

The largest rough (uncut) diamond is the Cullinan Diamond, which weighed **3,106 carats.**

FOSSIL FUELS

Long-dead plants and animals have been turned into materials that have been used as fuel for thousands of years. These fuels include peat, coal, and oil.

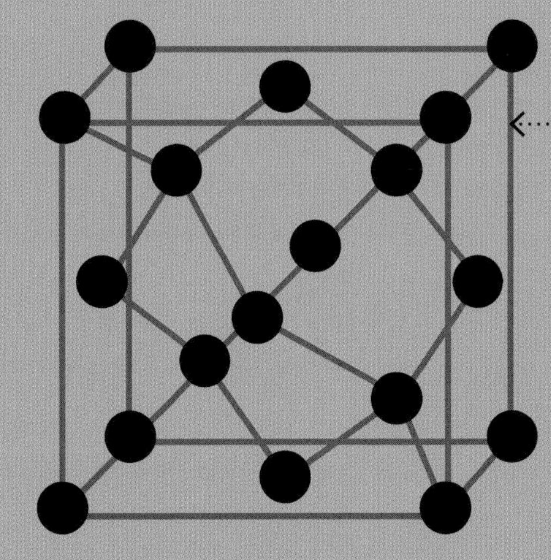

The strong bonds between the carbon atoms make diamond one of the hardest materials on the planet (see pages 22–23).

Carbon is vital to life on Earth. It forms the basis of all the tissues found in plants and animals.

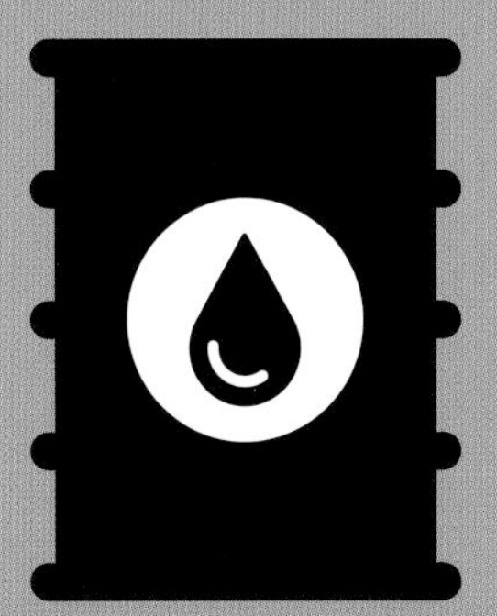

Every single day, about

100,000,000

barrels of oil are taken out of the ground around the world (a barrel of oil holds 42 gallons).

NANOMATERIALS

Carbon atoms can be arranged to form tiny cluster shapes called fullerenes. These can be ball-shaped or formed into tiny nanotubes. They can also be shaped into thin sheets called graphene, a material that's 200 times stronger than steel and can conduct electricity faster than copper. Graphene is being used to develop mobile phones that can be worn like a wristwatch.

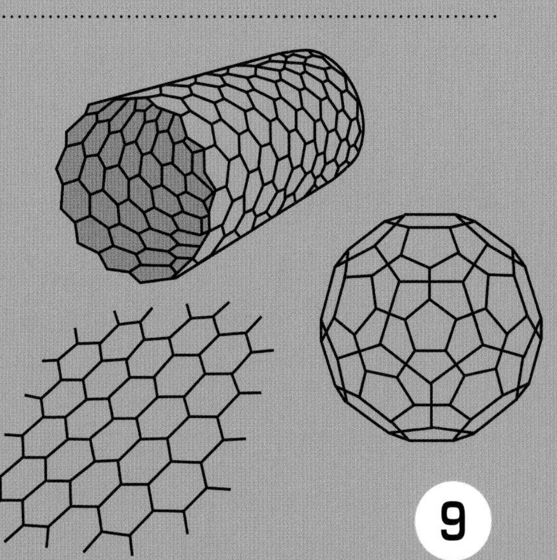

LIQUIDS

Liquids can flow and will take on the shape of anything they are poured into, but they will have a fixed volume and cannot be compressed.

Inside a liquid
The bonds between the particles are very loose, allowing the particles to move around.

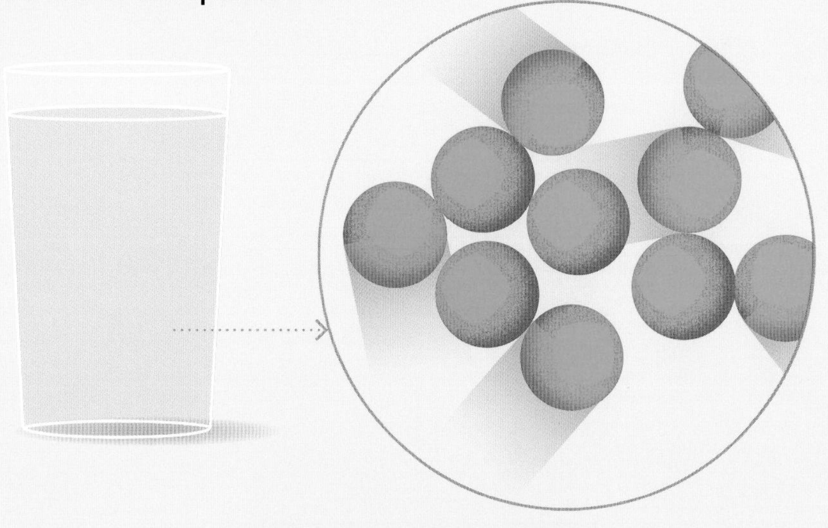

Moving particles

In 1827, scientist Robert Brown was studying pollen grains in water. He noticed that the pollen grains were moving, but could not work out how they moved. The pollen grains were, in fact, being pushed around by the water molecules as they moved about. This movement is called Brownian motion.

Pollen grain

Water molecule

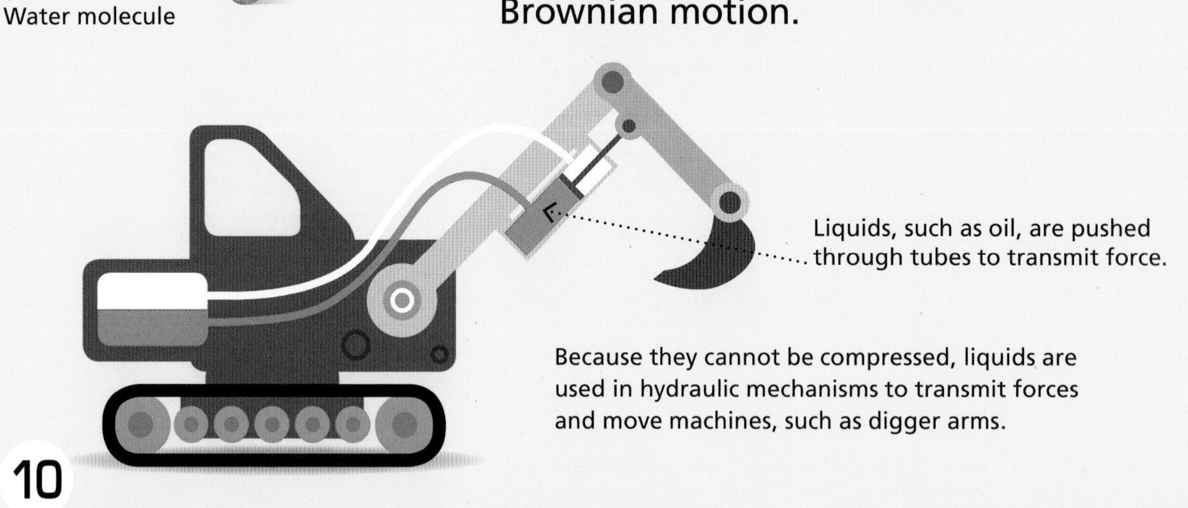

Liquids, such as oil, are pushed through tubes to transmit force.

Because they cannot be compressed, liquids are used in hydraulic mechanisms to transmit forces and move machines, such as digger arms.

Cohesion

Cohesion is the attractive force between particles of the same substance. This can create surface tension on the surface of liquids, creating a "skin" of particles that are more attracted to each other than the air above them.

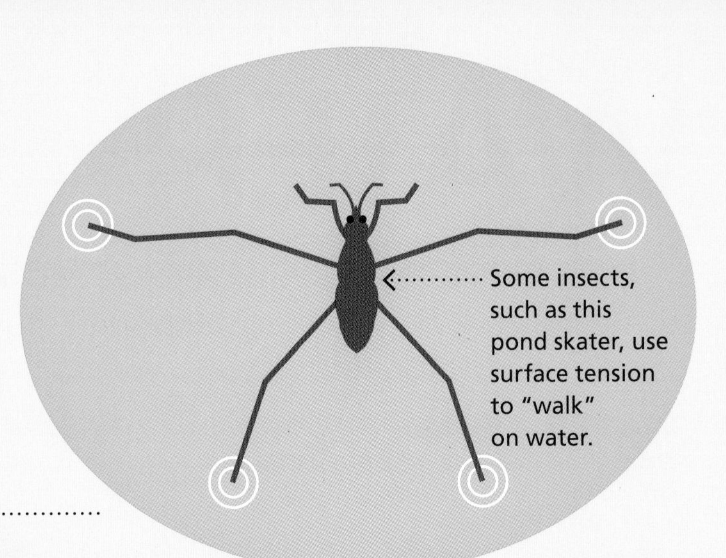

ADHESION

Adhesion occurs between particles of different materials. Liquid particles are usually attracted to the particles that make up the container holding them. This creates a slightly curved surface to the liquid, called a meniscus.

Meniscus

Water

Glass tube

ADHESION PRODUCES CAPILLARY ACTION, WHERE LIQUIDS ARE DRAWN UP THIN TUBES. TREES USE CAPILLARY ACTION TO CARRY WATER HIGH INTO THE AIR, MORE THAN 328 FEET (100 M) IN THE TALLEST TREES.

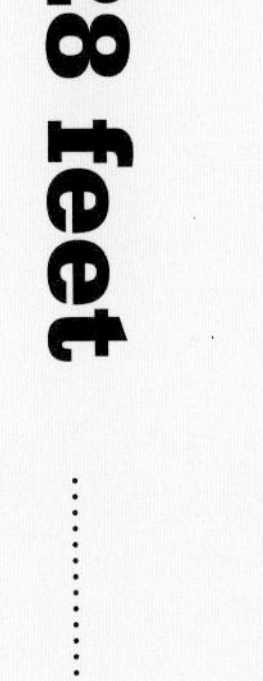

Pitch-drop experiments are some of the longest-running experiments in the world. They record how long a thick liquid, such as bitumen, takes to form a drop. One experiment in Brisbane, Australia, was started in 1927 and recorded its first drop in 2000, about 73 years later.

Thick and thin

How easily a liquid moves is called its viscosity. Water has low viscosity and flows easily, while honey has high viscosity and flows slowly.

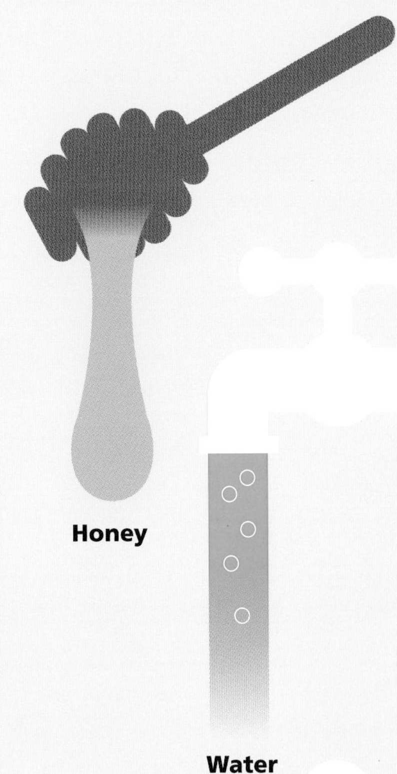

WATER

Water is the most common liquid on the planet and is the only substance that naturally exists in solid, liquid, and gas states on Earth.

WATER CYCLE

Water flows from one state to another and around the planet in the water cycle.

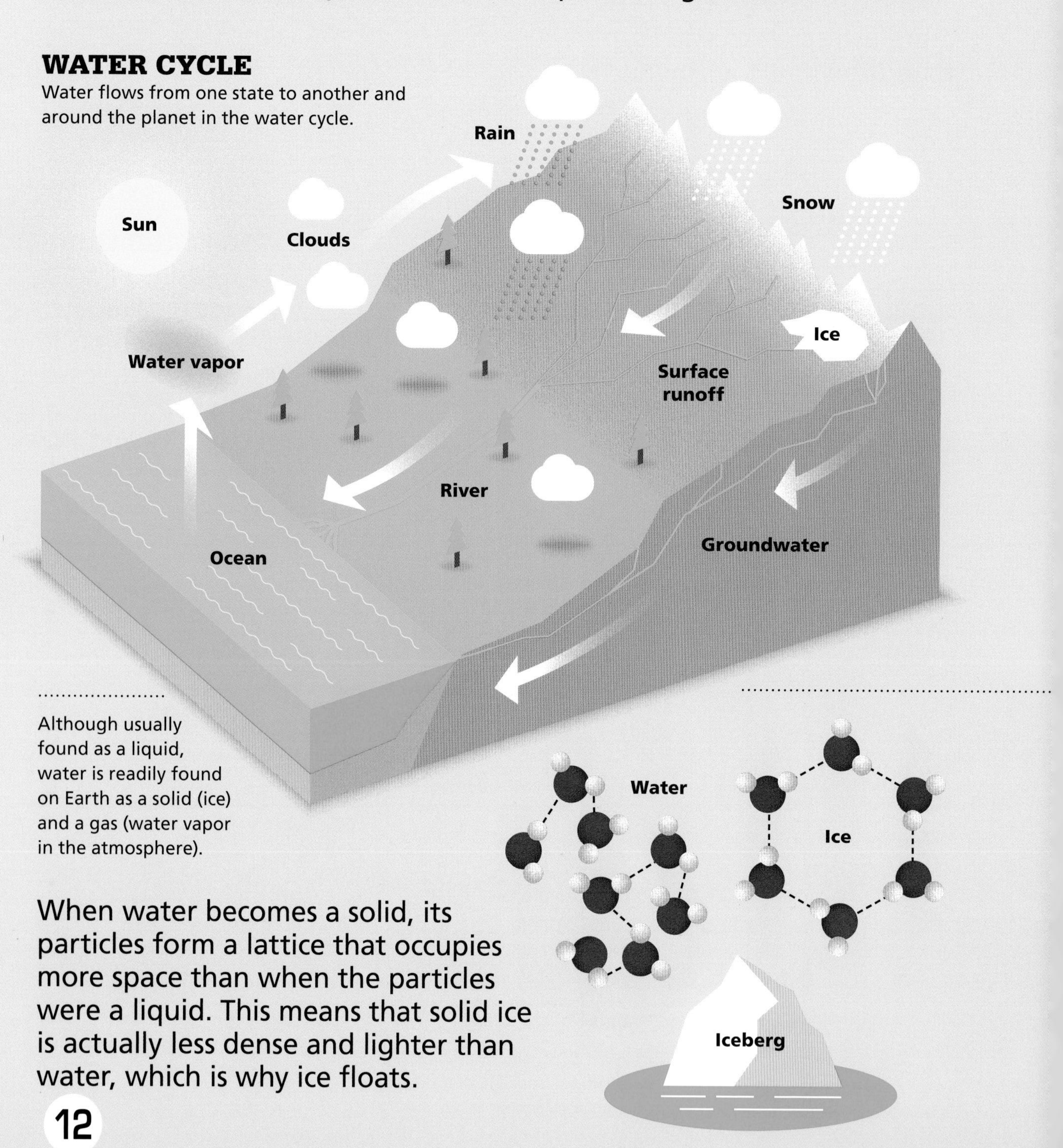

Although usually found as a liquid, water is readily found on Earth as a solid (ice) and a gas (water vapor in the atmosphere).

When water becomes a solid, its particles form a lattice that occupies more space than when the particles were a liquid. This means that solid ice is actually less dense and lighter than water, which is why ice floats.

WATER IS ESSENTIAL TO LIFE:

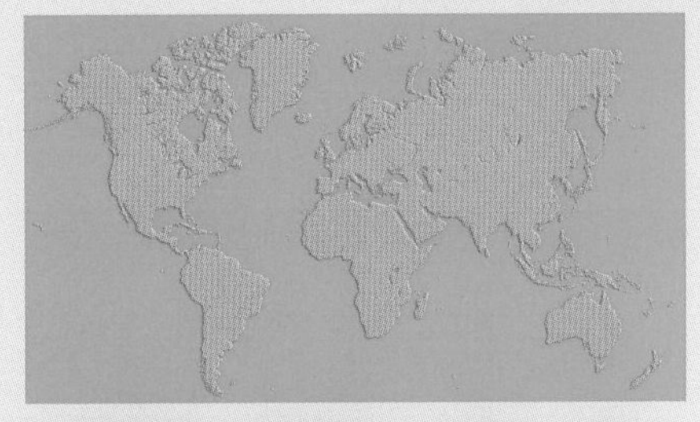

70%

Water covers about 70 percent of our planet's surface.

75%

About 75 percent of a living tree is made up of water.

60%

About 60 percent of an adult human's body is made up of water.

52.8 MILLION GALLONS

– THE AMOUNT OF WATER USED EVERY SECOND TO GROW FOOD FOR THE PLANET.

The amount of water on the planet doesn't change, which means we're drinking water that the dinosaurs drank more than 66 million years ago.

Ice

Water

Water expands by about 9 percent when it freezes. This produces so much force that it can burst water pipes.

Water found in the seas and oceans is known as salt water.

Salt water contains **35 grams** of minerals for every liter of water.

GASES AND PLASMAS

Unlike solids and liquids, gases do not have a set volume and can expand to fill any space. As gases expand, the particles that make them up get farther and farther apart.

INSIDE A GAS

The bonds between the particles that make up a gas are very weak and they move around freely. The particles are far from each other and arranged randomly.

Gases expand to fill the container that holds them and they can be compressed.

NITROGEN 78%

OXYGEN 21%

ARGON 0.93%

CARBON DIOXIDE 0.038%

OTHERS (including neon, helium, and krypton) **0.032%**

THE ATMOSPHERE IS A MIXTURE OF ABOUT 15 GASES.

The atmosphere is a layer of gases around Earth. It stretches up about **300 miles (**500 km) into space, getting thinner the higher you climb.

Some gases, such as **hydrogen** (H) and **helium** (He), are less dense than air.

Tungsten hexafluoride is one of the heaviest gases known, and about **11 times heavier than air.**

Fill a balloon with hydrogen or helium and it will rise.

Fill a balloon with this and it will drop like a stone.

Gases can be squeezed into small spaces. Pumping up bicycle tires pushes more air into them, increasing the pressure inside and making them hard. This makes cycling around much easier.

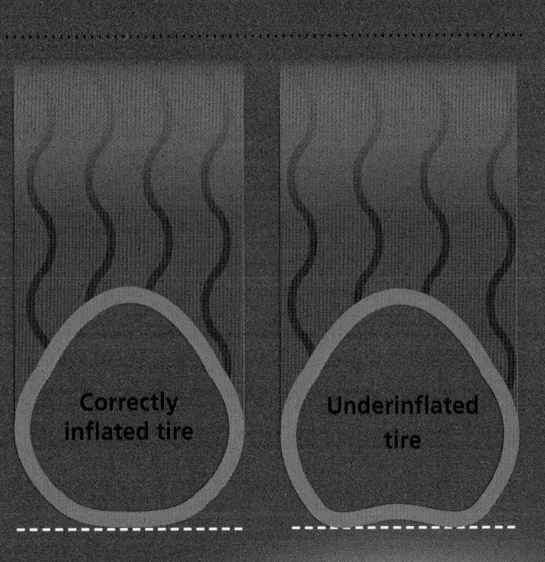

WHAT IS A PLASMA?

Plasmas are similar to gases, but their atoms have been stripped of most or all of their electrons, leaving positively charged nuclei. However, they behave in such a different way from gases that they are considered a fourth state of matter.

Plasmas are found in plasma globes and stars.

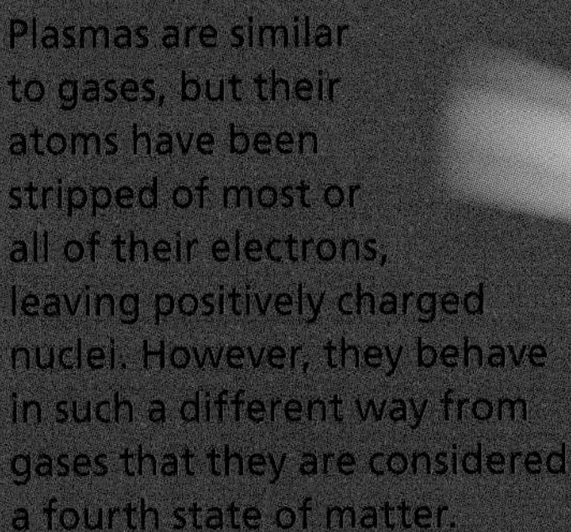

HYDROGEN

Hydrogen (H) is a colorless, odorless gas, but its amazing properties make it one of the most important elements in the universe.

Hydrogen is the most common element in the universe, making up about 75 percent of its mass.

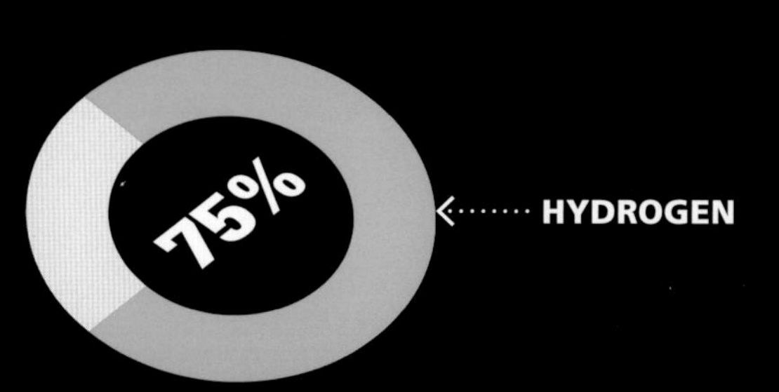

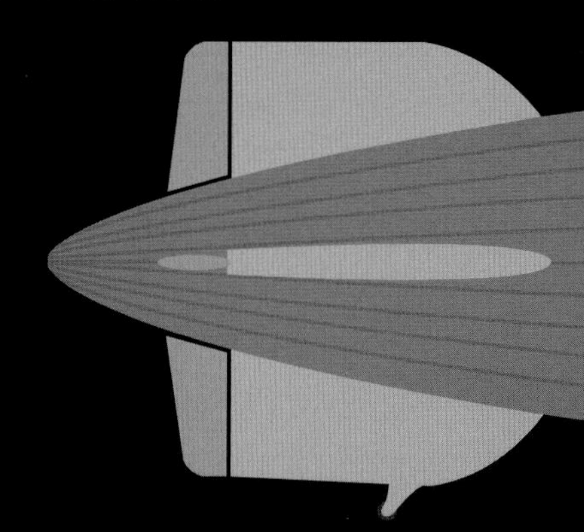

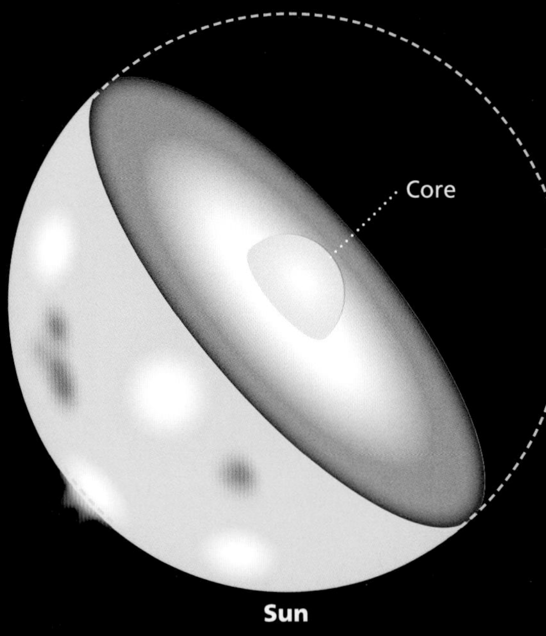

Deep in the core of the sun, enormous pressures and temperatures fuse hydrogen nuclei together to form helium nuclei. This process releases huge amounts of energy, which we experience as light and heat.

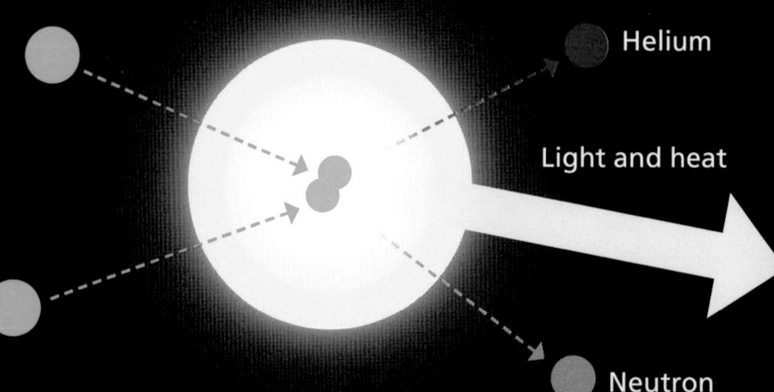

Scientists believe that all the other elements in the universe were formed by fusing hydrogen atoms together or fusing together other elements made from hydrogen atoms.

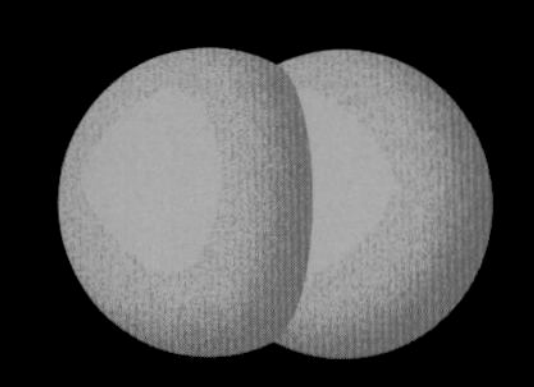

AS A GAS, TWO HYDROGEN ATOMS BOND TOGETHER TO FORM A MOLECULE.

ON MAY 6, 1937, THE GERMAN AIRSHIP *HINDENBURG* BURST INTO FLAMES AS IT TRIED TO LAND AT LAKEHURST, NEW JERSEY, KILLING 36 PEOPLE (35 ON BOARD AND ONE ON THE GROUND).

HYDROGEN FUEL CELLS ARE SEEN AS A POLLUTION-FREE ALTERNATIVE TO FOSSIL FUELS, SUCH AS OIL. **THEY ONLY PRODUCE WATER VAPOR.**

HYDROGEN IS USED TO POWER ROCKETS THAT BLAST OFF INTO SPACE.

Hydrogen is the only element that can exist without **neutrons.**

MELTING AND FREEZING

Moving from one state to another requires a change in temperature. Changing from a solid to a liquid is called melting, while changing from a liquid to a solid is called freezing.

Adding energy as heat to a solid causes the particles to vibrate more vigorously, weakening the bonds between them so that they move freely as a liquid.

ADDING ENERGY → **WARMER**

Solid

Liquid

COOLER ← **REDUCING ENERGY**

Cooling a liquid reduces the energy of the particles and they vibrate less vigorously. The bonds between particles become stronger and they form a solid.

Melting point – the temperature at which a solid becomes a liquid.

MELTING

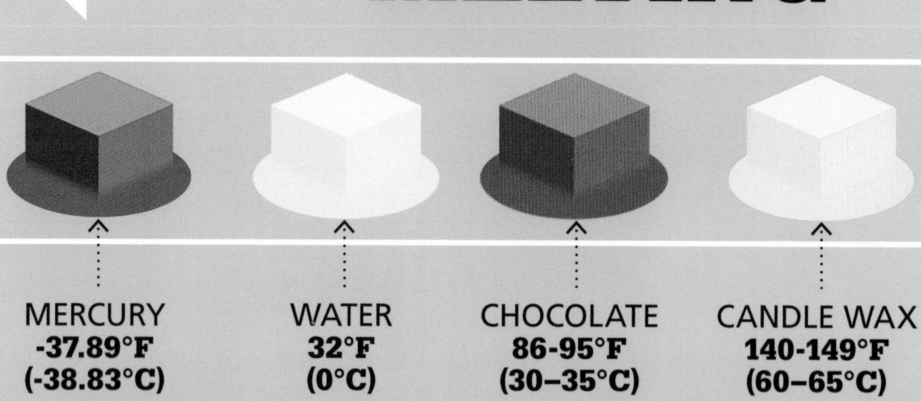

MERCURY
-37.89°F
(-38.83°C)

WATER
32°F
(0°C)

CHOCOLATE
86-95°F
(30–35°C)

CANDLE WAX
140-149°F
(60–65°C)

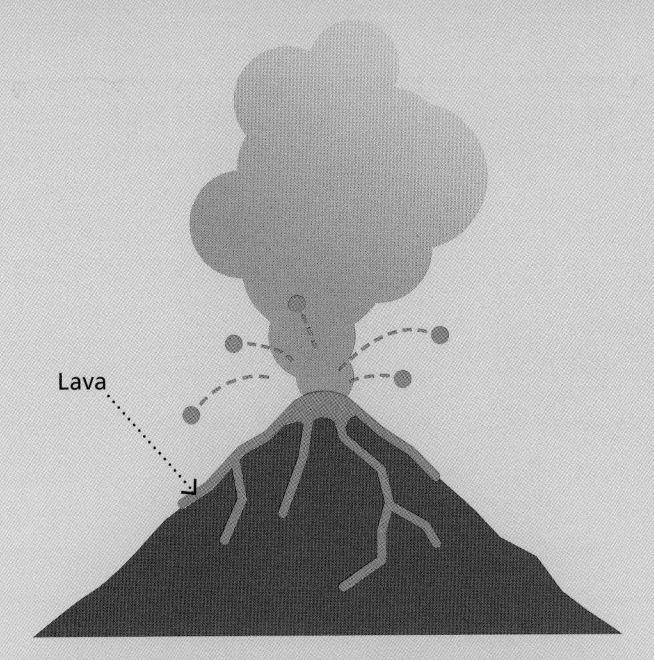

Rocks far below Earth's surface are heated so much that they melt to form liquid magma. When this is pushed out onto the surface in a volcanic eruption, this liquid rock is called lava.

1,300–2,280°F

THE TEMPERATURE OF LAVA

Melting ice sheets
Changes in global temperatures have a great effect on the polar ice caps. Scientists predict that if global warming continues, then the Arctic could be ice-free in summer by 2040.

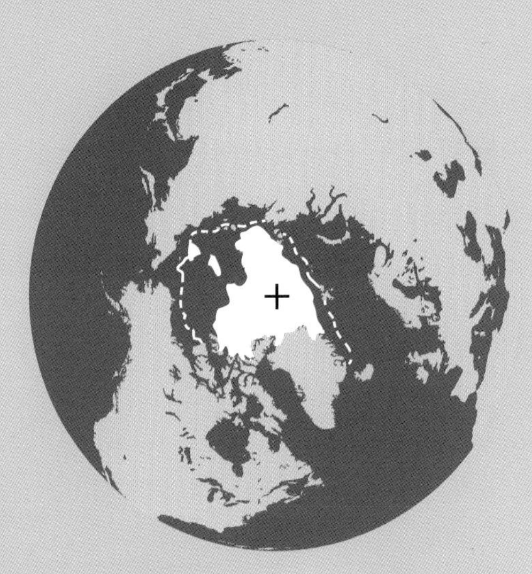

Most substances freeze and melt at the same temperature. Agar, however, melts at 185°F (85°C) but solidifies at 88–104°F (31–40°C).

POINTS

BOILING AND CONDENSING

Changing from a liquid to a gas is called boiling, while changing from a gas to a liquid is called condensing.

Adding energy as heat to a liquid causes the particles to vibrate more vigorously, weakening the bonds between them even more so that they fly around at random as gas particles.

ADDING ENERGY → **WARMER**

Liquid

Gas

Cooling a gas reduces the energy of the particles and they vibrate less vigorously. The bonds between particles become stronger and they come together to form a liquid.

COOLER ← **REDUCING ENERGY**

Boiling point – the temperature at which a liquid becomes a gas.

BOILING

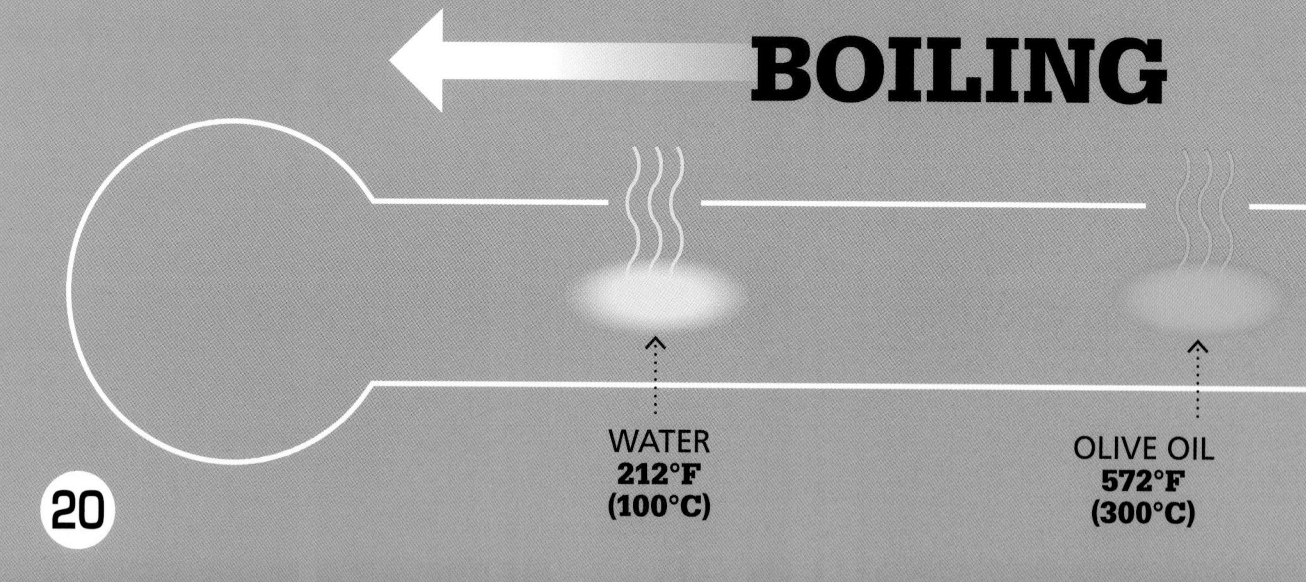

160°F

AFFECT OF AIR PRESSURE

212°F

The boiling point of something changes with air pressure. For example, at the summit of Mt. Everest (29,029 feet), air pressure is lower and the boiling point of water drops to 160°F (71°C).

Boiling point of salt water

Adding salt to water increases its boiling point to 216°F (102°C), but it will heat up faster and boil quicker than pure water.

SUBLIMATION

Some chemicals turn from a solid to a gas without melting into a liquid first. This process is called sublimation. These chemicals include arsenic, iodine, and carbon dioxide, which sublimates from its solid state (also called dry ice) to a gas at -109.3°F (-78.5°C).

–109.3°F

Dry ice

DEW

When water vapor in the air cools, the water particles come together to form droplets. These droplets create clouds, or, if they occur close to the ground, they can cover the surface of objects with dew.

POINTS

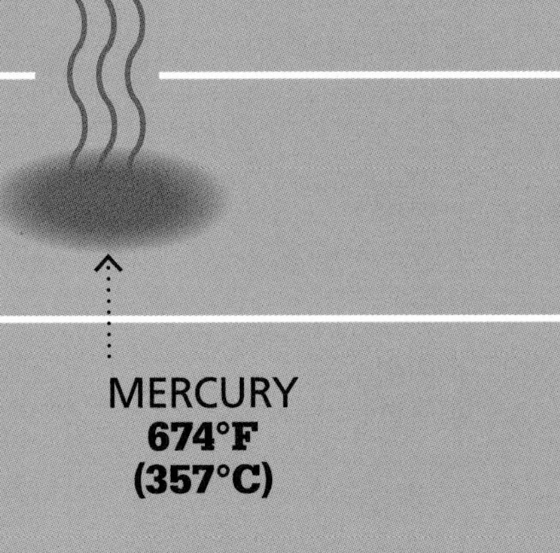

MERCURY
674°F
(357°C)

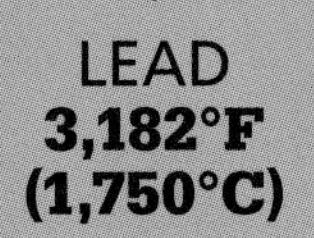

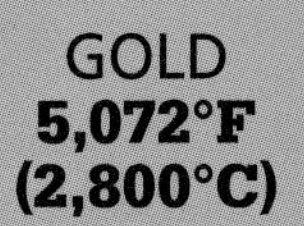

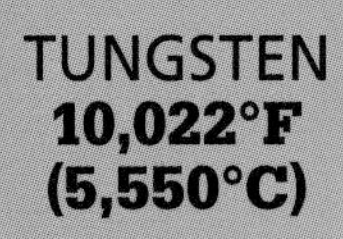

HARD AND SOFT

Different materials have different properties. They may not look and feel the same, and could be suitable for various roles. One of the properties scientists use to define materials is how hard or soft they are.

INCREASING

MOHS SCALE

Scientists measure the hardness of objects using the Mohs scale. This uses different minerals as a guide to hardness, from the softest, talc, to the hardest, diamond.

1

TALC

In its powdered form, talc is known as talcum powder.

2

GYPSUM

Gypsum is a soft mineral and one form, alabaster, has been used to make sculptures.

2.5

FINGERNAIL

3

CALCITE

Calcite forms clear crystals, and fine-grade calcite was once used to make weapon sights for targeting.

3.5

COPPER COIN

4

FLUORITE

Fluorite crystals are usually colorful, but clear fluorite is sometimes used to make lenses for microscopes and telescopes.

HARDNESS

5

APATITE

Apatite is a source of the chemical phosphorus and is used to make fertilizer.

5.5

KNIFE

6

ORTHOCLASE

Orthoclase is sometimes used to make glasses and ceramics, such as porcelain. It is also found in the gem moonstone.

7

QUARTZ

Quartz is a common crystal and one variety includes the gemstone amethyst.

8

TOPAZ

Topaz is usually colorless, but small impurities produce the range of colors found in topaz gems.

8.5

MASONRY DRILL BIT

9

CORUNDUM

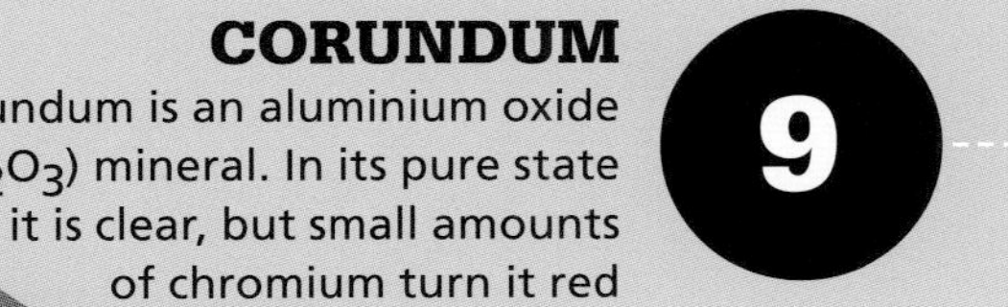

Corundum is an aluminium oxide (Al_2O_3) mineral. In its pure state it is clear, but small amounts of chromium turn it red to form ruby, while small amounts of iron and titanium turn it blue to form sapphire.

10

DIAMOND

Diamond is four times harder than corundum. It is used in jewelry, but also in cutting tools and drills.

WURZITE BORON NITRIDE is actually harder than diamond, but it needs the super-high temperatures and pressures of a volcanic eruption to create it and very little exists naturally.

PLASTIC AND ELASTIC

Materials can be classified on how they react when a force is applied to them – will they bend and stretch and then return to their original size, or will they take on their new shape permanently?

ELASTIC DEFORMATION
– when a force changes the shape of a material, but the material can recover its original shape when the force is removed.

PLASTIC DEFORMATION
– when a force changes the shape of a material permanently.

Spoon

Elasticity

A steel bar can stretch elastically for about **0.01 times** its length.

Natural rubber will stretch about **five or six times** its length.

Scientists have created a hydro-gel (a gel with particles that spread throughout water) that can stretch **up to 20 times its length.**

×20

Elastic objects can store potential energy if they are stretched. This energy becomes kinetic energy when the object is released, such as when a catapult launches a projectile.

GLASS

Some materials, such as glass, are very brittle and can break easily. However, when glass is heated to a high temperature, it can change shape easily and has been used to make a wide range of objects for thousands of years.

Blowing air into a lump of red-hot glass produces a hollow chamber, which can be shaped to make a vase, a bottle, or a drinking vessel.

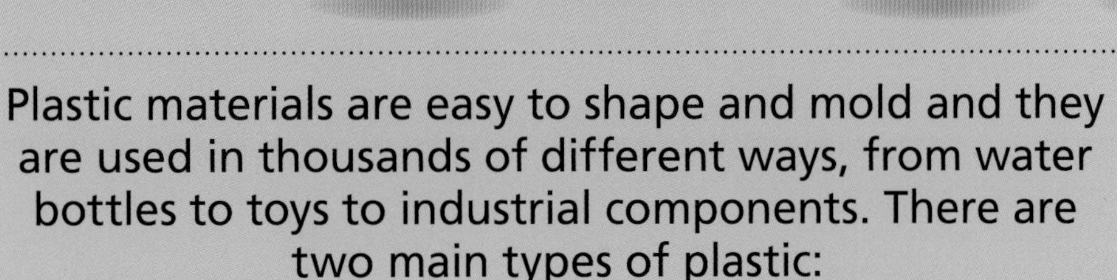

Plastic materials are easy to shape and mold and they are used in thousands of different ways, from water bottles to toys to industrial components. There are two main types of plastic:

THERMOPLASTICS

– can be heated and shaped many times. They include:

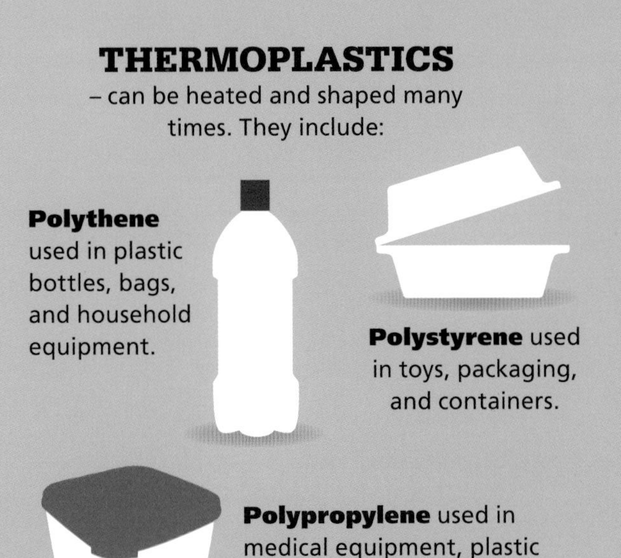

Polythene used in plastic bottles, bags, and household equipment.

Polystyrene used in toys, packaging, and containers.

Polypropylene used in medical equipment, plastic seats, kitchen equipment.

THERMOSET PLASTICS

– can only be heated and shaped once. They include:

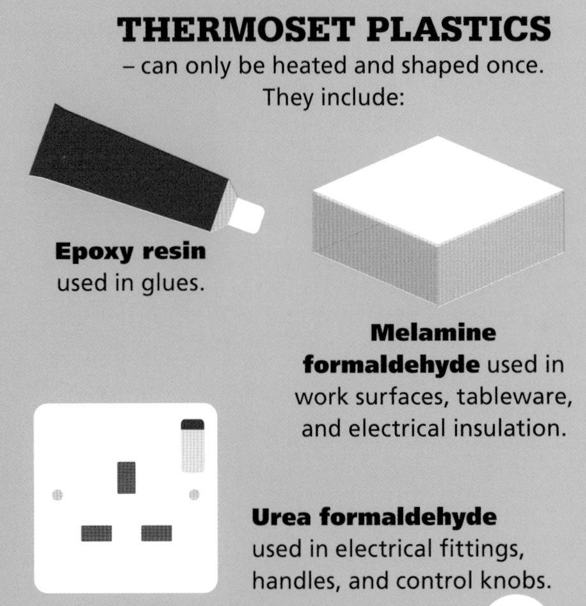

Epoxy resin used in glues.

Melamine formaldehyde used in work surfaces, tableware, and electrical insulation.

Urea formaldehyde used in electrical fittings, handles, and control knobs.

ACIDS AND BASES

Liquids can be classified on their acidity, or how they react to other substances. The level of acidity includes acids at one end of the scale and bases and alkalis at the other. While these substances can be very dangerous if they are strong, they have many important everyday uses and some play a vital role in keeping us alive.

PH SCALE

The strength of an acid or a base is measured using the pH scale. This goes from 0 for a very strong acid to 14 for a very strong base, with 7 as neutral.

pH	Substance
0	Battery acid used in a car
1	Stomach acid
2	Lemon juice
3	Soda
4	Tomato juice
5	Black coffee
6	Urine (average)
7	Pure water

Acids

Detecting acids and bases

Scientists use special indicators to detect whether a substance is an acid or a base. The indicator changes color, becoming red for a strong acid or dark purple for a strong base.

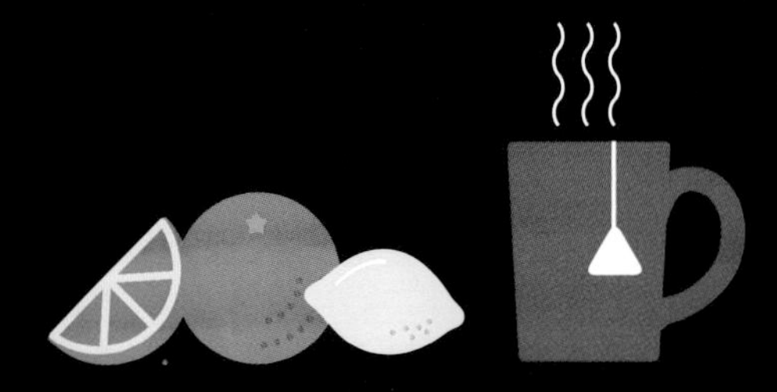

EVERYDAY ACIDS

Carbonic acid found in fizzy drinks
Tannic acid in tea
Citric acid in citrus fruits (oranges and lemons)
Ethanoic acid in vinegar

Your stomach contains **hydrochloric acid,** which helps to break down the food you eat. Too much of this acid, however, produces indigestion.

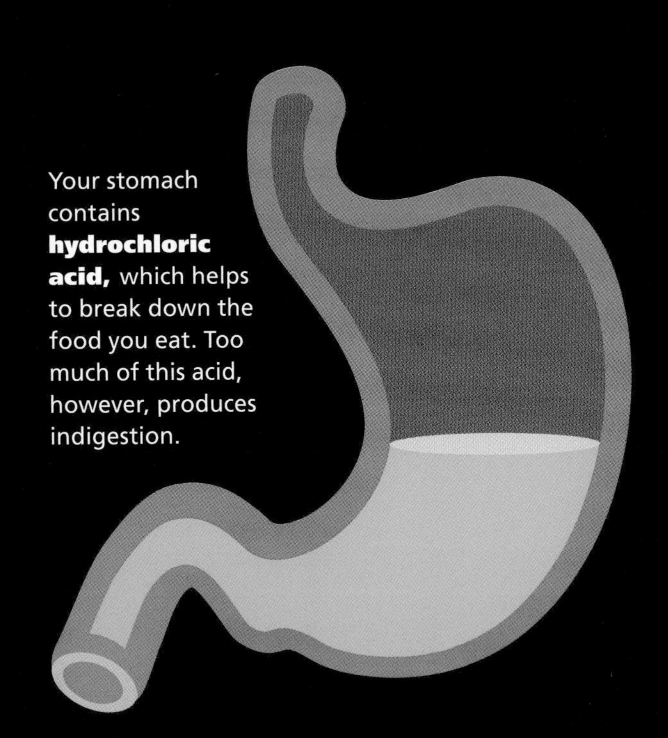

MAKING THINGS NEUTRAL

Mixing together an acid and a base produces a reaction called neutralization. The end result of this reaction is the production of a salt and water. For example, mixing together sodium hydroxide with hydrochloric acid produces water and sodium chloride, better known as table salt.

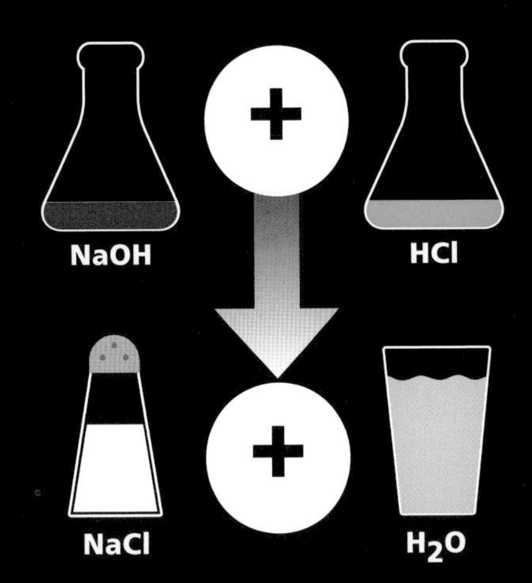

Seawater	Baking soda	Antacid tablets	Soap	Ammonia	Bleach	Drain cleaner
8	9	10	11	12	13	14

Bases

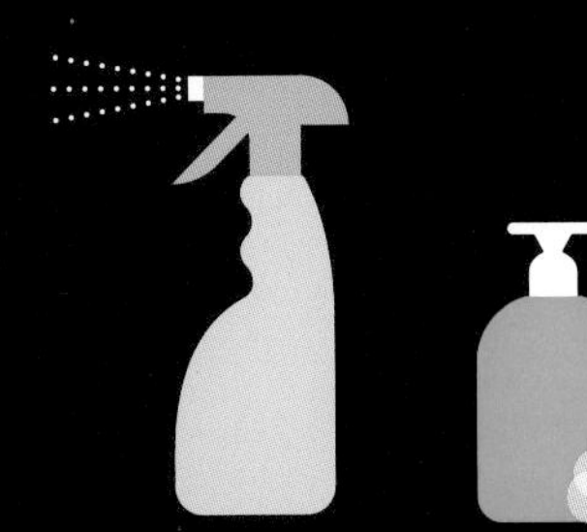

COMMON BASES

Ammonia used in household cleaners

Soap

FARMERS SPREAD CALCIUM OXIDE, OR LIME, ON A FIELD TO NEUTRALIZE ACIDIC SOILS SO THAT CROPS GROW BETTER.

MIXTURES AND COMPOSITES

Mixtures are formed when two or more substances are mixed together without reacting with each other. Substances are also combined to form new and very useful materials.

SOLUTIONS

When they are mixed with water, some substances dissolve. They look like they have disappeared, but they have mixed with the water to form a solution.

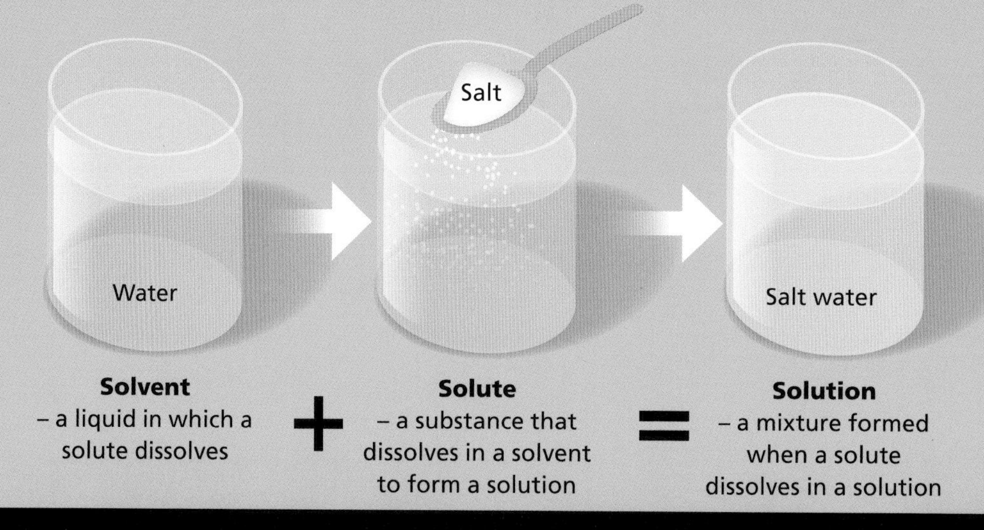

Solvent – a liquid in which a solute dissolves + **Solute** – a substance that dissolves in a solvent to form a solution = **Solution** – a mixture formed when a solute dissolves in a solution

Separating

There are several methods for separating substances that have been mixed together. The method used depends on the properties of the individual substances and how they have mixed together.

Filtering
When an insoluble solid is separated from a liquid by pouring the mixture through filter paper.

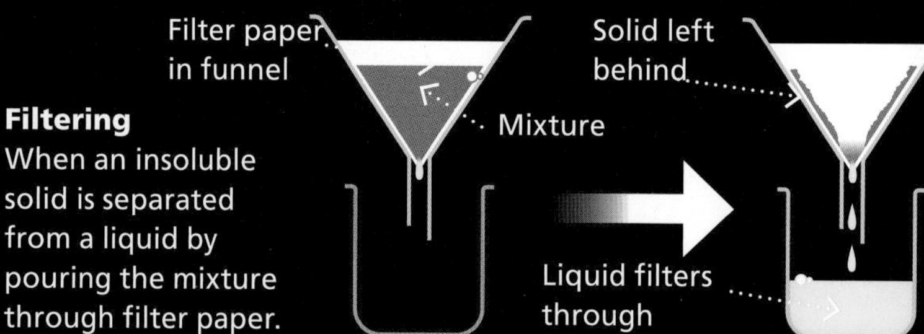

Evaporating
Used to separate a soluble solid from a liquid. During the process, the liquid evaporates, leaving the solid behind in the container.

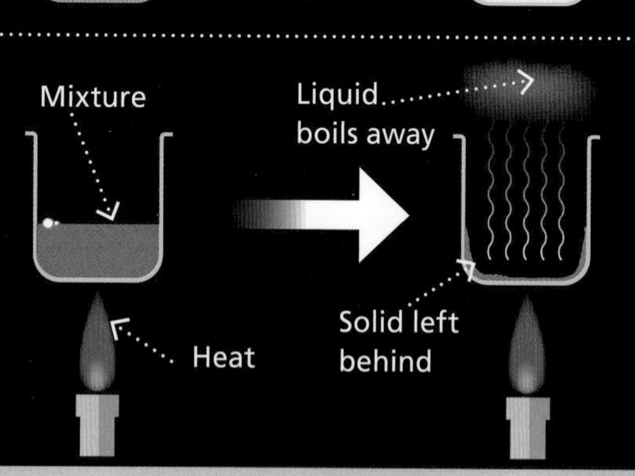

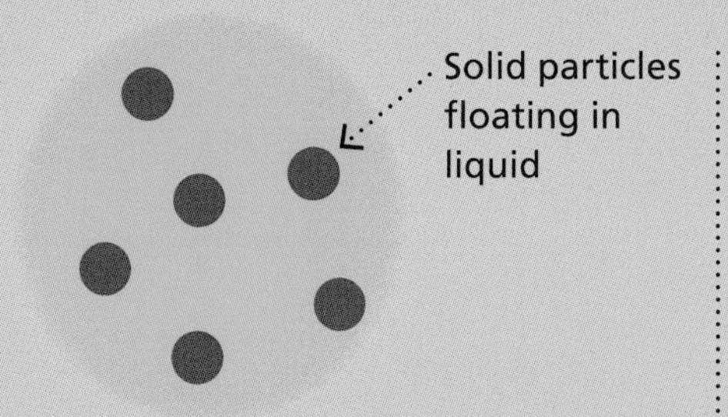

SUSPENSIONS

A suspension is a type of mixture in which the solid does not dissolve into the liquid. Instead, small particles of the solid float around and they may separate out if they are not mixed regularly.

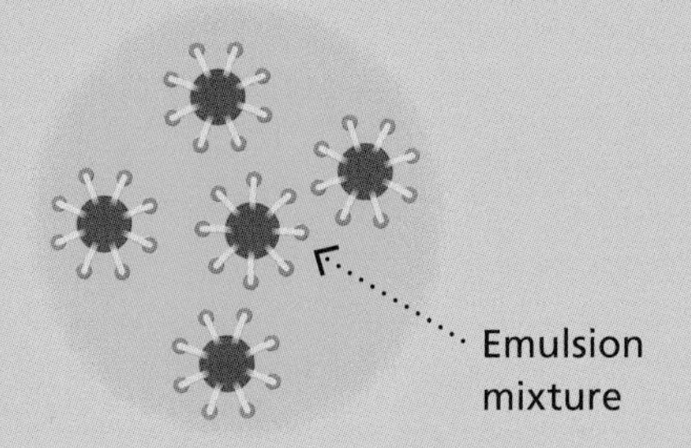

EMULSIONS

These are formed by two liquids that won't dissolve but are mixed together. For example, when oil and water are shaken together, tiny droplets of oil spread throughout the water.

Centrifuge

Used to separate solid particles in a suspension. The rapid spinning pushes the solid particles to the bottom of the container where they can be separated easily.

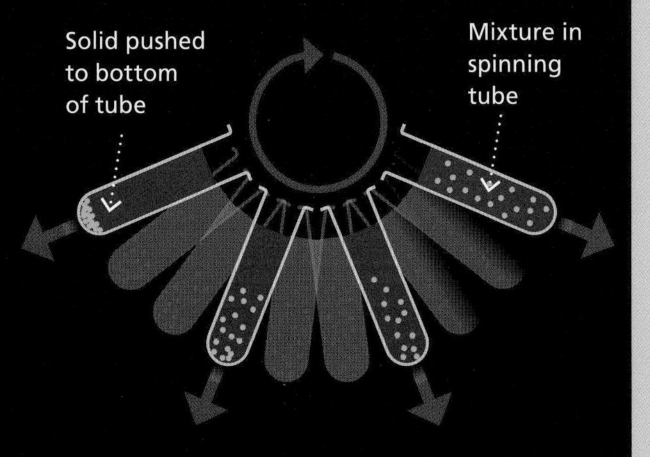

Composite materials

These are made from two or more different substances with the aim of creating a new material that performs better than its separate ingredients.

CONCRETE

Concrete is formed from a mixture of cement, sand, gravel, and water. It can be poured like a liquid, but will harden to form a super-tough, rock-like material.

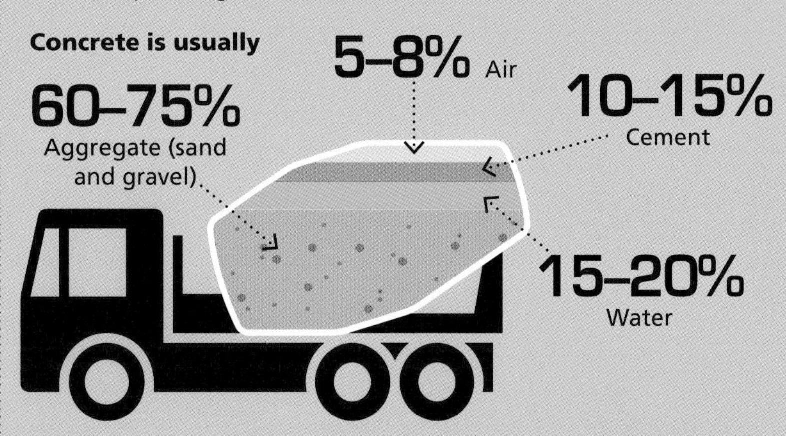

The Romans were using concrete about **2,000 years ago** to make some of their most impressive buildings, such as the Pantheon and the Colosseum in Rome.

CARBON FIBER

This material is made up of fibers of carbon. These fibers are set into a resin to form a lightweight but strong material that can be used to make a wide range of objects, including cars and boats.

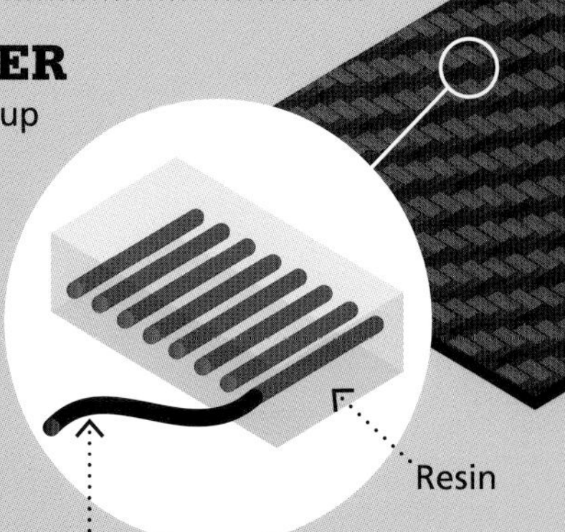

GLOSSARY

acid
A highly reactive liquid that can dissolve some substances.

alloy
A mixture of metals or a mixture of a metal with another element, such as carbon.

atom
A basic building block of matter, made of electrons, protons, and neutrons.

base
A substance that reacts with an acid to produce water and a salt.

boil
To change state from a liquid to a gas.

ceramic
A nonmetallic solid that does not conduct electricity and is not easily dissolved by acid. Clay and sand are examples of ceramics.

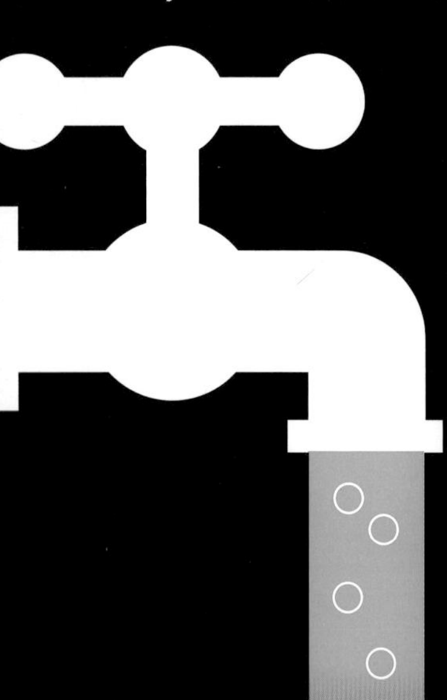

compress
To squeeze something into a smaller space. Gases can be compressed, while solids and liquids cannot.

condense
To change state from a gas to a liquid.

crystal
A solid made of atoms or molecules arranged in a regular pattern.

elastic
A property of a solid in which it changes shape when a force is applied to it, but returns to its original shape when the force is taken away.

electron
A negatively charged subatomic particle.

element
A form of matter containing just one kind of atom.

fossil fuel
A fuel, such as coal, oil, and gas, that is found in the earth. Fossil fuels are formed from the remains of ancient animals and plants.

gas
A state of matter in which the bonds between particles are very weak, meaning that a gas has no fixed volume.

liquid
A state of matter in which the particles are weakly bonded to one another. A liquid is fluid, meaning that it has no fixed shape, but has a fixed volume.

metal
A grey, shiny material that easily conducts electricity and heat. Most metals are solids at room temperature.

mineral
A solid found in nature with a crystalline atomic or molecular structure.

molecule
A particle of matter that contains two or more atoms bonded to one another.

neutron
A subatomic particle with no electric charge.

nucleus (plural nuclei)
A dense region at the center of an atom, containing protons and neutrons.

pH
A measure of the acidity of a liquid.

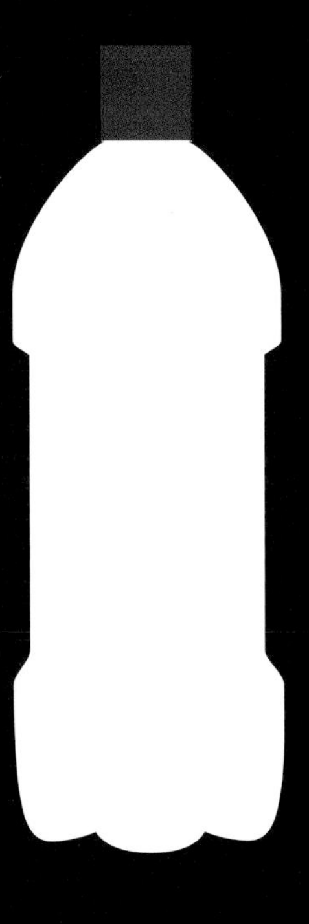

plasma
A highly energetic state of matter in which electrons have separated from the atoms' nuclei. Most of the visible matter in the universe is in the form of plasma.

plastic
A property of a solid in which it takes on a new shape when a force is applied to it, and keeps this shape after the force has been removed.

proton
A positively charged subatomic particle.

salt
A neutral chemical that is produced by the reaction of an acid with a base.

solid
A state of matter in which the particles are strongly bonded to one another to form a fixed shape and volume.

subatomic particles
The particles from which atoms are made. These are electrons, neutrons, and protons.

sublimate
To change state directly from a solid to a gas without first becoming a liquid.

water vapor
The gaseous form of water, produced by the boiling or evaporation of liquid water.

Websites

MORE INFO:
www.chem4kids.com/
This website has facts and figures about the chemical reactions that take place all around us.

www.dkfindout.com/us/science/solids-liquids-and-gases/what-is-matter/
This page includes a lot of information on matter, atoms, and molecules.

MORE GRAPHICS:
elearninginfographics.com/category/k12-infographics/elementary-school-infographics/
This web page has tons of school-related infographics.

www.kidsdiscover.com/infographics
This website contains a whole host of infographic material on many different subjects.

Publisher's note to educators and parents: Our editors have carefully reviewed these websites to ensure that they are suitable for students. Many websites change frequently, however, and we cannot guarantee that a site's future contents will continue to meet our high standards of quality and educational value. Be advised that students should be closely supervised whenever they access the Internet.

INDEX